THE NAKED
GARDENERS

Happy Naked Gardening

with best wishes from Barbara

THE NAKED
GARDENERS

ABBEY HOUSE GARDENS

Picture Credits

All photographs in this publication were taken by Ian and Barbara Pollard except pages 20 and 37 (Mark Bolton); 84 and 90 (Barry Novis); front cover, half title, frontis and pages 10, 80, 89 (Alexandra Papadakis); pages 8 and 94 (Rob Peel); title page and page 78 (Bec Wingrave)

Design Director: Alexandra Papadakis
Editor: Sheila de Vallée

First published in Great Britain in 2006 by
PAPADAKIS PUBLISHER
An imprint of New Architecture Group Limited
16 Grosvenor Place
London SW1X 7HH
020 78 23 23 23
www.papadakis.net

ISBN 1 901092 59 3

Printed and bound in Singapore

Contents

Looking from the Saxon Archway in April the rose beds are awash with tulips including the varieties Happy Generation, Dreaming Maid, Margot Fonteyn, Monsell, Gudoshnik, Candeal, Brigitta and Madame Lefeber.

Abbey House Gardens
Malmesbury, Wiltshire

Dove Bend

Camellia Walk

Camellia Walk

MONASTIC
FISH POND

The Stump

MONASTIC
FISH POND

RI
A

St. Aldhem's Pool

FERNERY

WATERFALL

MIL

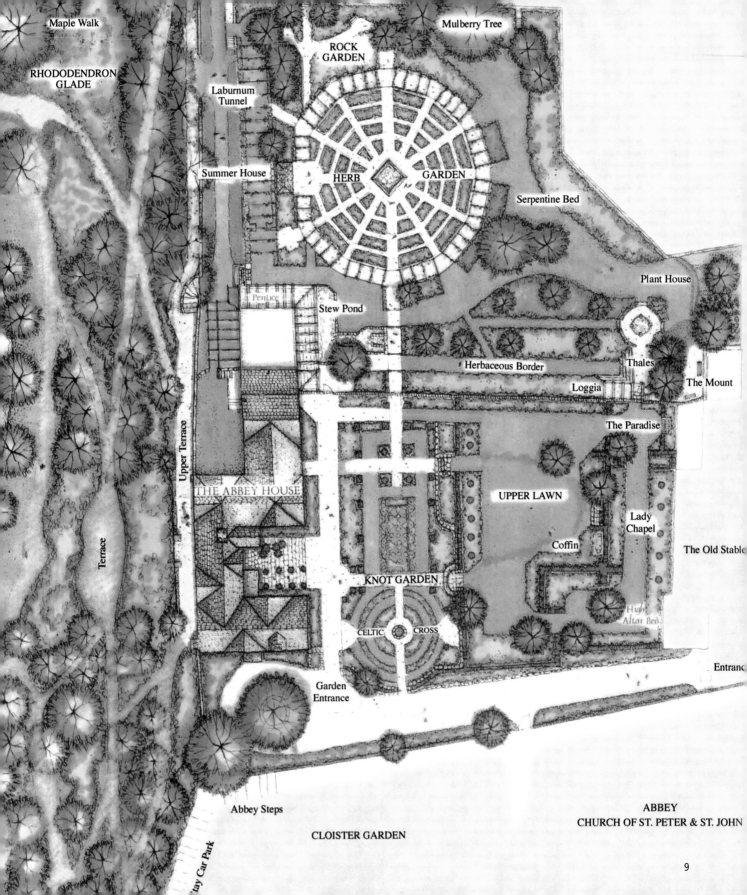

Maple Walk

RHODODENDRON
GLADE

ROCK
GARDEN

Mulberry Tree

Laburnum
Tunnel

Summer House

HERB   GARDEN

Serpentine Bed

Plant House

Pentice

Stew Pond

Herbaceous Border

Thales

The Mount

Upper Terrace

Loggia

The Paradise

THE ABBEY HOUSE

UPPER LAWN

Lady
Chapel

Terrace

Coffin

The Old Stable

KNOT GARDEN

High
Altar Bed

CELTIC   CROSS

Garden
Entrance

Entranc

Abbey Steps

CLOISTER GARDEN

ABBEY
CHURCH OF ST. PETER & ST. JOHN

ay Car Park

9

When Ian and Barbara Pollard arrived at Abbey House in 1994, Malmesbury opinion was not all in their favour, some inhabitants fearing that the sixteenth-century property in the heart of the town had been bought by 'a middle-aged hippy and his moll.' They were certainly a colourful pair. He, long haired and bearded, enigmatic and intellectual, was the possessor of an eclectic wardrobe. What little of it he wore rarely conformed to local sartorial expectations. She, a vision of red-streaked hair, multi-coloured fingernails and deliciously sexy clothing, set tongues wagging and Abbey House was marked down as a potential hotbed of debauchery and vice long before the first hot beds of summer were planted in the gardens.

It all ensured that from the outset rather more people than usual were interested in what went on there. Scenarios were imagined that the Pollards might have been tempted either to live up to or to live down. In the event they did neither, and their own scenario for Abbey House would prove much more fascinating and infinitely more colourful than anything the minds of Malmesbury might devise.

Ian has always been interested in wildlife, buildings, and gardens. He grew up in Cambridge, in his grandparents' council house where one year a peach tree produced over a thousand fruits and was the local wonder of the moment. His father, an air reconnaissance pilot was killed, aged twenty-three, during the Second World War, before Ian was born in 1945 and only fifteen months after his parents' marriage. Thereafter Ian grew up surrounded by five adults: his grandmother, mother, two aunts, and a grandfather often drunk in charge of a bicycle. An uncle turned him into a birder, encouraging him with a book on ornithology, and by the age of ten Ian had a collection of goldfish, catfish, tropical fish, seed-eating, caged birds

Ian and Barbara Pollard in the Laburnum Tunnel. Late May

that threw millet husks all over the floor, and a terrapin that was fed rather smelly raw meat.

When the aunts left home, his grandmother took in lodgers (mostly operators at the Cambridge telephone exchange where his mother worked) whom Ian was required to take round the college buildings at weekends, thus fuelling other interests: architecture, plants and landscaping. (In his opinion the backs of the Cambridge colleges are one of the true, man-made wonders of the world).

It became a lucrative interest. People started to pay him for the tours; college porters allowed the young boy admission to the buildings and Americans who tagged along sometimes gave him half-a-crown a head, so that he sometimes pocketed two pounds.

Learning how building sites were run and how tradesmen worked came with school holiday jobs: Ian was prepared to climb rooftops to help survey the Cambridge colleges, on one occasion hurtling towards the ground but saved by a parapet. That moment revealed two truths about the future man: surveying would be his career route into architecture, and he was clearly a risk taker.

The chief surveyor for Cambridge University Estate Management, Dick Stafford-Smith, was also a governor at The Purse School where Ian, having forged his mother's signature on a permission slip, took the entrance exam and was awarded a scholarship. Dick singled him out and absorbed him into the University Estate Management Department, teaching him the basic economics of buildings, quantity surveying and importantly, how to think like a client.

Ian's understanding of urban landscaping began at twenty-one when he was involved with multi-unit, small-scale housing designed by the architect Eric Lyons and he became aware that planting schemes had the potential to significantly affect the quality of life of the whole community. For a while he was involved in the logistics and planning of new urban village development, had brief periods i

eft: The view towards Malmesbury Abbey across the Formal Gardens. July

View of the Saxon Archway from the Celtic Cross Knot Garden. April

a sales and letting agent, then became a director of a property development company. At twenty-six he bought a Ferrari, moved his wife and two children into a six-bedroom farmhouse in Nottinghamshire, and decided to work for himself.

He was already organising funding for developments, negotiating as on-site contractor and setting up his own construction company to ensure total control. Soon he had two Ferraris but needed to move to a more accessible location if his development work was to go national.

Hazelbury Manor was a Grade I listed, fortified fifteenth-century gabled manor house with 180 acres near Box in Wiltshire. In 1972 it was a girls' finishing school with gardens, maintained but not developed, from the time of a previous owner John Kidson, who had laid them out with magnificent beech walks and sizeable yew topiary along the edges of a two-acre sunken lawn.

Basing his company headquarters at Hazelbury, Ian decided to create there a garden worthy of the house. He designed garden rooms with yew hedges, planted conifers and heathers around the entrance gates, fashioned a now famous yew topiary 'chess set', a ring of standing stones, and a laburnum tunnel. Over the next twenty years he transformed eight acres into formal gardens on a grand scale; traversed the landscape with an arboretum of thousands of trees, streams and lakes; planted a yew representation of Stonehenge to the correct orientation within concentric circles of sweet chestnut; and transported thousands of tons of soil to form two huge, prehistoric-like tumuli.

Gardening had become a consuming passion. He was seriously studying plants and how to care for them, an on-going process for a man whose uncompromisingly hands-on approach amazes most visitors to Abbey House Gardens today, where he has become both an inspiration and a gardening guru.

He was persuaded to open Hazelbury to the public to raise funds for Box parish church and from 1987 it opened regularly under the

The Scottish Gateway. July

Dutch and Tall Bearded Irises in the Celtic Knot Garden. May

Fountain in the Herb Garden. July

National Gardens Scheme. This not only gave pleasure to the numerous visitors but also ensured that his garden staff, of which by then there were eight, received recognition for their efforts.

In the period before the recession of the late 1980s Ian's award-winning company was phenomenally successful. But changes were in the air. The economy collapsed and he was forced to sell the house. He began to feel that his gardeners led a more satisfying life than his own. Whilst his hands were tied in legal bondage in London theirs were deeply rooted in the good earth of Wiltshire, which was where he really wanted his to be. Also he had met Barbara, and the mutual attraction was immediate. The relationship between them developed with all the speed of a breathless bodice-ripper.

Barbara Haworth, the daughter of a teacher and a nurse, who were both from farming backgrounds, was brought up surrounded by a three-acre garden in Lancashire.

Her parents' love of roses coloured Barbara's young life: she would weed between the plants but lost pocket money if she could not name them. At Abbey House Gardens, where over two thousand roses were planted to mark the Millennium, naming all of them would prove a formidable task.

Even when she was a student the links were forming that would bind her to Ian Pollard: she had a gardening background, and loved art, architecture and history. The family grew vegetables, ran a smallholding of a thousand chickens and kept a goat.

Barbara yearned for a garden when she did not have one. When in London, where she trained as a teacher, she moved around for fifteen years without putting her hands in the soil. She taught teenagers who had difficulty with English and learnt to type in order to produce material more suited to their needs. She wanted to be a better teacher and felt she needed more worldly experience. She therefore gave herself five years in which to do as many different jobs

as possible. She quickly learned that other jobs were far less stressful and much more lucrative. She did not go back to teaching.

Ten years later she had been a fashion model, a showroom executive for a fashion house, sold cloth to the fashion industry, carried out product promotion, worked in advertising and filled in the gaps temping with her typing skills. After a little travelling she was involved with a residential property development, realised she had become a Jack-of-all-trades, and that she could probably do anything if she put her mind to it.

But London had lost its appeal. She would return to Lancashire; more a night owl than a lark she thought of indulging her love of music by opening a piano bar. But Lancashire in the early 1980s was not ready for such a project.

Moreover, Barbara was no longer in step with Lancashire. Bath suited her better with its architecture and culture, and the glorious countryside surrounding it. A single visit determined her future and she moved there almost at once, knowing no one, with no job and initially no place to stay. But, armed with her typing skills and with the experience of teaching remedial children embedded in her curriculum vitae, she applied for a vacancy with a nearby property developer – Ian Pollard.

Seeing Hazelbury Manor on a spring day with its tapestry of heathers, daffodils and narcissi took her breath away. It was in total contrast to the fast living in cramped conditions that was London. Ian's business was exciting; the job was varied and drew on many of her interests and much of her previous experience. In Ian she found a strong and charismatic personality who usually made things go his way.

The recession brought the Pollards to Abbey House. They were negotiating to buy a property south of the M4 motorway when a friend mentioned a house in Malmesbury, similar in style to Hazelbury, with five acres of grounds crying out for a creative gardener. It had their name all over it and immediately caught their interest.

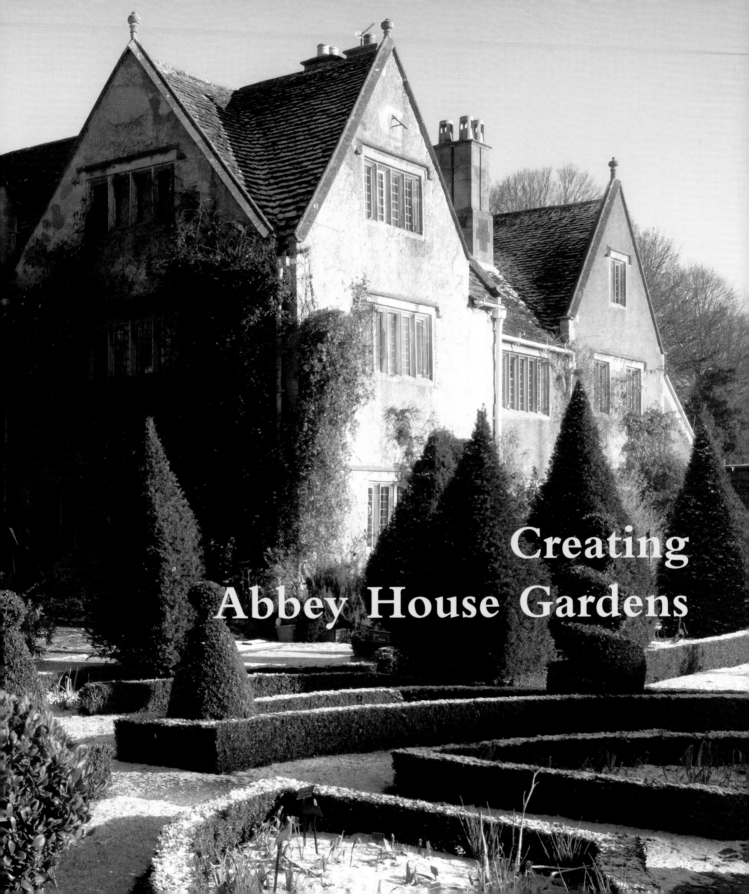

Creating
Abbey House Gardens

T he Pollards fell in love with Abbey House as soon as they saw it in 1994. It is right next to Malmesbury Abbey in the centre of the town but tucked away behind the Market Cross so that even many locals did not know it existed. And with its five acres of land it had huge potential.

At that time the garden was unremarkable. The house was screened from the drive by a mixed hedge of hawthorn, elder and sycamore, and an iron gate led to the front garden where four beds of roses, already long past their best bloom-by date were succumbing to disease and neglect. The rest of the front garden, historically the precinct of the Abbot, was tidy but the narrow perimeter borders were of little horticultural interest and the lawns once intended for croquet or tennis were now better suited to the study of mosses.

An old orchard beyond a brick-faced stone wall had a few fruit trees. Many were top heavy, suffering from honey fungus and surrounded by a sea of dandelions, tall sedges and low tussocks of coarse grass. A shelter belt of lime trees separated this area from the other half of the garden, which sloped steeply down to the river. Totally neglected for all of twenty-five years it was a wasteland, an untidy jungle of ivy, dead trees, nettles, brambles and all the pernicious weeds that are the nightmare of every gardener. But here too there were mature trees, which with judicious pruning would provide a fine framework, and Ian had always wanted to garden a slope to water.

With trees came birds. Ian spotted not only flycatchers but also a pair of tree-creepers, unusually working the same tree. The birder in him responded, 'If it's good enough for them it's good enough for me.' The scene was set and the relatively small size of the gardens meant that the Pollards could develop them together. They would be private gardens for their three children, except for occasional open days under the National Gardens Scheme.

previous page: The Formal Gardens in winter
Photo: Mark Bolton

left: The 16th-century Abbey House across the Celtic Cross Knot Garden in summer

Along the top lawn border wall a profusion of roses includes Anna Ford, Constance Fettes, Crathes Castle, Honeymoon, Memory Lane, Radox Bouquet, Rosy Future, Shirley Spain and Stacey Sue, with Clematis Vyvyan Pennell, and Lonicera x tellmanniana Honeysuckle. June

That was before Ian chaired Malmesbury's Millennium bid. Spurred on by the bureaucratic nature of its failure he took the decision to turn his gardens into a major tourist attraction. If the Millennium Commission was disinclined to understand Malmesbury's potential, he would show how wrong it was. A combination of the television programmes 'Meet the Ancestors' and BBC 'Gardeners' World', plus acclaim from gardening and leisure magazines would prove him right.

Local interest groups fundraising for good causes had been exerting increasing pressure for the gardens to open to the public on their behalf. Ian was at a watershed in his life: he could continue in property development; or he could become a full-time gardener. If he chose the latter he would need gardening help and there would have to be enough paying visitors to cover the development and the upkeep of the grounds, the house and everything associated with both.

The decision to make the gardens 'public' was taken in 1996. The aim was to have the structure completed for the Millennium. There was a great deal to do to meet Ian's naturally ambitious thinking processes but the renaissance was about to begin.

Ian is an instinctive and extremely visual gardener. His philosophy is that if a plant grows well where it is, then that is the proper place for it. If it does not flourish where it is, it is dug up, replanted if possible, and replaced.

The major intellectual influence on the gardens was the history of Malmesbury Abbey, which was also the main spatial influence. The gardens have been developed boldly, with a sense of scale and proportion commensurate with the Abbey church and its ruins as they are today. Visually, the arched sections of the great crossing contribute a magnificent backdrop to the upper gardens, and form an intrinsic part of them. Through Ian's vision the two properties again connect.

Yew cones amid Box swirls with Ornamental Cabbages. December

below: Bill Lazard's *Monk* contemplates
the Lady Chapel Garden

bottom: Stanchion of the Celtic Cross Knot
Garden from the east featuring Box, Purple
Berberis, Cotton Lavender, Wall Germander,
Lavender and Ripley's Gold Holly. August

The former site of the east end of the Abbey and its Lady Chapel is now picked out in yew, which at the same time compartmentalises the upper lawn area, adds privacy to the gardens, and achieves a dramatic sense of scale. A plan drawn up in the early 1900s by the late well-known local architect and archaeologist Harold Brakespear guided Ian's positioning of the hedge. To line it up perfectly with the existing Abbey he made use of ranging rods. Horrified local residents assumed that the ranging rods meant active construction and, without even asking for an explanation, reported Ian to the Council for illegal building work.

Further yew hedges were to 'replace' other historic stone walls and continue the divisions in the garden, which visitors would eventually be teased around. Ian is a master in leading the eye from one area to another by the careful creation of focal points to catch the interest of the visitor at just the right moment. But the detail would come later. There was basic work to be done immediately.

The ragged, mixed hedge bordering the drive was breached to reinstate the south porch as the point of entry to the house and new yew hedges were planted in wedges behind it to await a moment in their maturity when the old hedge could be removed to reveal along the drive deeper, more interesting beds that would act as a 'shop window' for the gardens.

To mark the Millennium Ian researched and planted more than two thousand different roses; to salute Maidulf, the Celtic monk who founded the first school on Malmesbury's ancient hill from which the monastery evolved, he designed and created a Celtic cross knot garden influenced by St Martin's cross on Iona.

Maidulf tutored Aldhelm, a member of the Wessex royal family, who subsequently received his Roman Catholic education at Canterbury, became the first abbot of Malmesbury, and was eventually canonised. Aldhelm walked on this land, played his lyre on the river banks, recited his poems to the audience attracted by his songs and

The Celtic Cross Knot Garden from the west with feature lollipops formed from Lonicera nitida, a ball of Buxus sempervirens and sempervirens variegata, Berberis thunbergii Atropurpurea Nana, Santolina chamaecyparissus, Teucrium chamaedrys, Lavendula angustifolia Munstead, Ilex Ripley's Gold. July

27

then educated them with stories of Christ. He bathed in the river that runs through the grounds and according to the writings of the historian, William of Malmesbury (a candidate for the remains found in the mediaeval stone coffin), 'That he might reduce the force of his rebellious body he used to immerse himself up to the shoulders in a spring near the monastery. There, caring neither for the frosty rigour of winter nor the mists rising from the marshy ground in summer, he used to pass the night unharmed.' In honour of the saint there is a spot in the river that was used as recently as the early 1900s as a place of baptism.

The knot garden was planted mainly with traditional knot garden plants – santolina, teucrium and box – but for contrast something from today – dwarf berberis – was added to give colour, depth and texture. It was planted up with iris, aquilegia and lily along with muscari, hyacinth and pansy.

Over the next four years, with the help of just one gardener, Martin Roberts, paths were lifted, repositioned and relaid, and herbaceous borders formed with mounds of soil to better show off their occupants. A laburnum tunnel – lighter, airier and with more comfortable proportions than the one Ian had created at Hazelbury – was underplanted with a succession of seasonal bulbs.

The borders were increased in size and number and densely planted to ensure dramatic impact with a kaleidoscope of seasonal colours. All available walls were clothed with climbers and vines. Roses scaled the mature trees in the river gardens and were planted in all shapes, sizes and colours as standards, teas and miniatures.

An unusual herb garden was created and planted up within an encircling colonnade to support 180 fruit cordons of apple, pear,

The Courtyard with Parthenocissus turning red on the house walls, with Wisteria and Euonymous. Phormium and Pelargoniums in pots. October

White Rose Coopers Burmese above the red Parkdirektor Riggers behind Kniphofia Royal Standard and Northiae, with roses Glorious and English Miss in the forefront. June

quince, medlar and grape vines on the outer circumference with climbing roses and clematis on the inner face. The whole area measures 100ft in diameter, contains raised oak beds for a collection of herbs, and is centred on a fish pond with a fountain.

Next to a two-hundred-year-old mulberry tree and behind the herb garden, the ground was cut away to form a gully where ornamental plants would be seen to advantage at eye level by the passing visitor.

Ian built a plant house to over-winter exotics and converted old, ugly workshops into a belvedere – a pleasing shelter from the rain that could also be used for exhibitions.

He created a covered walkway with a seating area for refreshments, a large stew pond, an ornamental pond, waterfall and fish ponds to bring water, light, reflections and life.

In the river gardens the work was yet more arduous: he had to build a bridge, install an irrigation system to help establish young trees, create compost bins, build new paths to create better access, terracing for the back slopes, new gates and fencing – and everything had to be done in time for the Millennium.

It was a massive undertaking, all funded from the Pollards' own pockets. Not for them any further dealings with lottery commissions and the like. They would do it themselves to show what could be done with foresight, commitment, energy and determination. It was not easy; success was not guaranteed but it was Ian's firm belief that if you stay focussed and do not let anything sidetrack you or get you down, you cannot fail. It had worked for him before; it would work for him again. His determination, vigour and tenacity would see him through.

The Formal Gardens

Visitors enter through the formal gardens so immediate impact was required. The gardens had to be colourful to draw the eye from the all-too-often grey English sky but bold in scale and well structured to hold their own against the built masses of the late Tudor house and adjacent Malmesbury Abbey, the fabulous backdrop that informs every view. The design should reflect the 800 years that Benedictine monks had lived there but cross reference with the Tudor period, which saw the arrival of knot gardens and topiary as owners began to see their gardens as a source of pleasure as well as food production.

Roses Super Excelsa and Uetersen scramble over the Scottish Gateway leading through archways of Golden Hop into the Herb Garden. Early July

left: Some of the 440 varieties of Tulip including Arabian Mystery, China Pink and Dancing Show. Late April

The Formal Gardens with the Celtic Cross
Knot Garden and Saxon Archway

The proliferation of roses and Alstroemeria in the Formal Gardens, against the backdrop of Malmesbury Abbey

left: Everlasting Love Knot of Box and Wallgermander

below: The **Formal Gardens in winter** with Monk's Head of Yew

above: The **Celtic Cross Knot Garden** in winter. The patterns were inspired by Saint Martin's Cross on Iona

below: **Yew sentinels in the Formal Gardens**
Photo Mark Bolton

The Saxon Archway seen across the crown of the Celtic Cross Knot Garden with Irises surrounding the ancient well. May

Ian Rank Broadley's *Towards Another* seen
through the Saxon Archway

Bearded Iris from Richard Cayeux: Honky
Tonk Blues, Robe d'été, Afternoon Delight,
Alizes, and Jazz Fesitval May

Rosa Gallica Complicata behind roses
Fellowship and Ice-cream. June

The Herb Garden

Barbara thought the addition of herbs would improve family meals and suggested a few be grown near the kitchen door so that she could harvest the leaves at will. Ian liked the idea ... but not the location or the quantity. His solution was a sunken garden 100ft in diameter surrounded by a circular colonnade of fruit cordons separating the area from the herbaceous borders, serpentine bed, laburnum tunnel and stew pond, and containing oak sided raised beds, ideal for herbs that prefer not to get their roots wet. Sited in the former orchard, food production would continue where it had begun.

Roses Scarlet Showers, Elizabeth Heather Grierson, Rosy Mantel and New Dawn flowering above beds of Santolina chaemoecyparissus and varieties Lemon Queen and Viridis, with Artichokes, Phlomis Russeliana, Lavender Angustifolia Hidcote, and Malva Sylvestris. July

left: Roses Illusion, Bad Neuenahr and Coral Creeper growing through arches around the Herb Garden. July

Roses Sparkling Scarlet and My Love with Clematis Madame Edouard André, Ascotiensis and Etoile Violette, and Rosa Pink Perpetue adorn the arcaded walk. Raised oak beds contain varieties of Lavender, Alchemilla, Sanguisorba, Geranium, Origanum, Thymus, Verbena, and Salvia. July

The Green Man on the arcaded walk around the Herb Garden with Rosa Katie and Clematis Voluceau. July

Agastache Foeniculum in front of Alchemilla
alpina and Alchemilla Splendens in the Herb
Garden. July

Clematis Dr. Ruppel along the
Herb Garden arcaded walk. June

Herbaceous Borders

Earth scraped from the intersecting paths of the herb garden was deposited near by and inspired Ian to create mounded beds in the mixed double herbaceous borders. He laid a grass walk between borders to the west, and a gravel walk along the top of the borders to the east. By mounding the earth he was better able to show off the wide range of plants growing 3-4ft high. As the season progresses plants rise from the soil to a height of 6ft in some cases, screening visitors from each other as they stroll along the different paths.

Nepeta Six Hills Giant, Papaver Orientalis Beauty of Livermere, Lysimachia Firecracker, Verbascum Cotswold Queen, Cirsium Rivulare Atropurpureum. Late May

left: Deutzia gracilis Nikko, Papaver Orientalis Patti's Plum, Red Valerian. May

The Grass Walk looking towards the *Thales*
water sculpture by Barry Mason. May

Looking across the Herbaceous Borders to the
Abbey with Yucca, Phygelius, Phlox, Verbena
Bonariensis, Dahlia, Oenothera. October

The Gravel Path in the double Herbaceous Borders with Delphiniums, flowering Yucca, Hardy Geraniums, Alchemilla, Nepeta, Thalictrum, and Phlomis. June

The Laburnum Tunnel underplanted
with Aliums. May

The Gravel Path to the Round Pond in the double Herbaceaous Borders, with Alstroemeria, Hardy Geraniums, Verbascum, Thalictrum. July

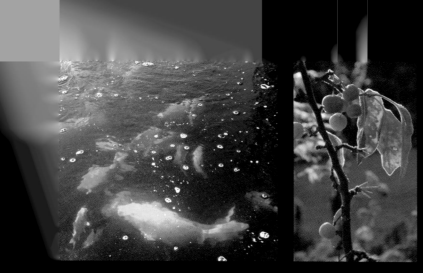

far left: **Koi Carp in the Stew Pond**

left: **Crab Apple Golden Hornet**

below: **The Stew Pond**

opposite: **Physocarpus Diabolo behind Rosa Fragrant Delight. June**

The River Gardens

Totally overgrown and neglected for over twenty years, this was the most challenging part of the garden for Ian but the part he most wanted to succeed. Sloping paths had to be cut into steep slopes but only after a plethora of pernicious weeds had been ripped from the ground – an ongoing story! It is a rewarding area to watch develop: mature trees form a natural framework for younger underplanting. A total contrast in scale, mood and microclimate it offers a complete change of scene, an opportunity to further encourage wildlife, and space for collections of specimen trees and shrubs.

Heather bank below the Middle Terrace in the River Gardens. March

left: The path to the River Gardens with the footbridge over the Avon. May

The River Gardens. May

Around the waterfall in the River Gardens.
October

Giant Tree Fern (Dicksonia antarctica) with
Hydrangea aspera var. Sargentiana, with its
neighbouring Teller hybrids H. macrophylla
Redstart, Spotted Woodpecker and Hostas.
August

Stepping stones across the River Avon to the
Fernery in summer

Rhododendron 'Rocket' and Azalea 'White Lady' beside the 'monastic fish ponds' in April with views to the north elevation of The Abbey House and to the mound with grasses and phormiums christened 'S-tumpe' by the Pollards after William Stump who built The Abbey House after 1542

Rhododendron and Narcissi in the
River Gardens. Late April

Becoming
The Naked Gardeners

The Naked Gardeners

The Pollards are not the archetypal owners of an historic house, who, when they have enough money, breathe a sigh of relief, build a wall, shut the gates and distance themselves from the rest of the community. They decided, even before exchanging contracts that if they succeeded in buying Abbey House, they would share with others this integral part of the town. If they were to create the kind of gardens Ian had in mind, he wanted people to enjoy what he had done. To him, there is no sense in spending one's life creating something beautiful only to hide it away. There was never any question of not allowing outsiders into the gardens, but rather how many, when, and how often.

In business terms, opening the garden was a gamble. In those days, there was nothing to draw people to Malmesbury other than to visit the Abbey but Ian and Barbara realised that if their plans worked, they might help put Malmesbury on the tourist map. which would be good for the town's economic health.

It is sometimes difficult for visitors to understand that this is still a private garden. Despite its huge public appeal and the great sense of belonging that thousands of people feel when they visit, the gardens at Abbey House are owned by the family that tends them, eats and plays in them in much the way that visitors do in their own garden. That the gardens are on a much larger scale than most is frankly irrelevant.

For this reason, when the gardens were opened for the first time in 1998 it was for just three days a week, with Ian and Barbara attempting to balance time spent with visitors and time spent with their family. They hoped to ensure that for part of the week they would have a garden they could call their own.

previous page: Ian and Barbara in the
Celtic Cross Knot Garden

left: Ian and Barabara in the Foliage Garden

word of mouth; and by the weather. They had not realised what a stimulus they themselves would quickly become. Most of the great gardens attached to historic houses were laid out by owners and plantsmen who have long departed this life, but here was a garden where the creators were both hands-on and accessible. The combination was compelling for both general public and the professionals.

Initially Ian and Barbara thought that professional gardeners would be a strong target market. The RHS, to which Ian belonged, invited its members to visit Abbey House at a special admission price, enclosing the Pollards' first piece of printed publicity: a leaflet Barbara designed and printed on their home computer. It did not bring in floods of people. Nor was the weather kind in that first year, always seeming to rain on their three opening days. If the business was to succeed, the garden had to be open to take advantage of fine weather. Not for the first time, a compromise was reached: they would close only on Mondays. But when the first Bank Holiday Monday was a scorcher, they realised that the only real answer was to open seven days a week throughout the season.

At first the general public only trickled in, having seen a poster for the gardens outside the gates. Barbara prepared a few words of introduction, donned a yellow shirt, hot pants, tights and a leather money belt and rushed out of the house to greet every stranger she glimpsed from the kitchen window.

There were many more lessons to be learnt.

The wet springs, summers and winters of 1998, 1999 and 2000 resulted in thousands of hyacinths rotting; squirrels chewed the tops off hundreds and hundreds of crocus, and freak gales blew over trees in full canopy to uncover honey fungus eating away at the roots. A neighbour's tree flattened new plantings of rhododendron; two crack willows simultaneously lost limbs that flattened bog garden planting; and just when it had all been

roots of bamboo, killing the trees and necessitating that replanting be cased in wire netting to allow creature and plant to cohabit. Neighbours' cats would pee on favoured plants or attack young birds, sometimes right in front of visitors. Plant labels, put in the ground before the master record was created, vanished into visitors' pockets, or were removed as part of a child's collecting game, or picked out by adolescent jackdaws in their 'pecking order' disputes, or simply tossed aside by blackbirds hunting for worms amid clumps of farm manure rotting down too slowly. Much larger labels had to be acquired and the task repeated with the additional cost and months of extra work involved in labelling more than 10,000 different plants. Herons stole fish, and electricity cuts compromised filtration systems with further loss of fish life.

Ian, under pressure to finish paths by his deadline pressed on in unfavourable conditions and nearly lost his digger and his life when his machine skidded at the top of the steepest slope. Luckily it wedged under a mature tree that broke what might have been a fatal fall.

But there were good things too.

From the earliest days visitors' comments were always positive and encouraging.

The wet years of the late 1990s created perfect conditions for the trees and shrubs to settle in well and make good growth so that maturity came sooner than might have been expected. Most of the planting flourished in the light, friable, alkaline soil that had been worked for centuries before its more recent neglect. And doubtless the fact that part of the ground had been the monks' graveyard, improved the quality of the soil as a growing medium.

In early 1997, during preparation of the rose beds, a mediaeval stone coffin was unexpectedly uncovered lying less than a foot below the surface at the head end, very close to the location of the former Lady Chapel. Judging by Ian's adjacent yew hedge, which mimicked earlier walls and whose position was based on drawings from the early 1900s by eminent architect and archaeologist Harold Brakespeare, the coffin lay as close to the high altar as possible without being inside the building – clearly a sought after position. The Pollards had undertaken a resistivity survey to avoid disturbing any historic remains but the coffin was not found until a border fork hit the stone and the beautifully carved sarcophagus came to light. It was large enough to contain a six and a half foot skeleton. Details of the find were broadcast far and wide with the result that a previously planned 'open weekend' to raise funds for the local primary school attracted 1,500 visitors. BBC 2 took an interest and created a programme on the find entitled 'The Rose Garden Mystery' in their 'Meet the Ancestors' series. Suddenly the Pollards were attracting media attention but they could not know where this would lead.

A well-known garden photographer, Clive Nichols, who had taken photographs of Ian's planting at Hazelbury Manor for a glossy magazine, was invited to the new gardens and some of his images were published in magazines such as *The English Garden* and *The Sunday Times Style Magazine*, generating much public interest.

Gradually visitor numbers were building up from 2,000 in the first year to 9,000, to 15,000, to 20,000. By now refreshments were wanted: a coach party of over thirty could not sit together in the small venues Malmesbury had to offer at the time, so tea was made available on site. Cakes were provided by an outside caterer and subsequently by one of the tea shops that later opened up near by. Barbara's mother Dora, who had come to live with the family, wielded the teapot with a ready smile and a warm welcome.

Future increases in numbers would necessitate a complete rethink of this side of the operation but not before another matter outside Ian and Barbara's control came to affect the overall picture.

Ian and Barbara tying in roses along the Upper Lawn Wall

Foot and Mouth, 2001

Most large gardens are located outside town centres, often near agricultural land, and in sympathy with the heartache affecting many farmers The National Trust closed its properties to the public. The National Gardens Scheme also asked owners not to open as planned until the epidemic was over. Many other well-known tourist attractions were forced to close.

Abbey House Gardens with its unique town centre location was never a threat to farming but public perception was that gardens were closed so visitors headed for the coast. During the spring visitor numbers dropped like the temperature. Things were looking grim.

But 2001 would turn out to be a very important year.

May brought not just the later flowering tulips, irises, laburnum and wisteria but Len Curswell, a researcher for BBC 'Gardeners' World'. Based at Pebble Mill in Birmingham Len was on his way to Dorset to feature a well-known rose garden for a programme 'special' on this ubiquitous plant. He would pass through Wiltshire and checked *The Good Gardens Guide* for other venues to consider. The first entry was Abbey House Gardens and he dropped by, met the Pollards, filmed a little of the gardens and a conversation with them. The result was to change their fortunes. The BBC filmed a year in the garden presented by Alan Titchmarsh. When the programme was broadcast in late June 2002 visitor numbers trebled overnight. The following year, helped by a memorably hot summer, Abbey House Gardens attracted 60,000 visitors.

The film crew visited every other month for a year. Alan later described his first meeting with Ian in his book *Trowel and Error*, 'Standing in the middle of a rose bed, his long glowing hair fastened back in a pony tail, his face adorned with a grizzled beard he wore a pair of knee length boots, and a pink silk jock strap. Nothing else.' On the film crew's last day the Pollards gave them a farewell dinner and it was then that the crew learned that Ian would have been much

happier with no clothes at all had he felt it was possible. A very wide range of subjects was discussed that evening but for some reason this was the one they passed on to the journalist who wrote about the garden special in the *Radio Times*. 'The Naked Gardeners' were born.

If you are looking for the non-naturist's stereotypical view of a nudist, you will not find it in Ian. He is too individualistic, too much of an entrepreneur to do the group thing; he also has too low a boredom threshold to be inactive for long. Quite simply he feels the heat more than most, likes to let the healing sun get to as much of his skin as possible, and is comfortable enough in his own skin to be unconcerned if it is seen by others.

It all began many years ago but the *Radio Times* brought it to public attention with the photographs illustrating 'Weeded bliss', the article introducing viewers to the 'Gardeners' World' programme.

In the 1960s Ian was single-handedly converting a large terraced house in Cambridge and had just lost his job. Having cast aside many sweat-soaked or torn garments during a particularly hot summer, he was down to his last items of clothing. Under pressure to finish, he took a calculated risk that neighbours in the overlooking flats might be out and thus not notice his naked body ferrying debris outside. Within no time there were faces at all the windows. It was too late to cover up; Ian bowed to the gallery and thereafter continued to work with no clothes, sustained by regular cups of tea from two elderly spinsters who lived next door, clearly not offended by his nakedness. In subsequent years his

The Naked Gardeners

world at Hazelbury grew accustomed to the sight of him, during the summer months, at work in the buff; but he would dress for meetings with the wider world.

But the wider world knew of his predilections, as Barbara learnt from the employment agency that sent her for her interview. She wasn't bothered so long as he didn't expect her to do likewise. But that would change. Ten years into their relationship she was persuaded to visit a naturist beach in Dorset and although she felt extremely self-conscious for the first ten minutes, that was all it took to change her perspective. At Abbey House she would be perfectly comfortable pursuing various activities *au naturel*.

Both Ian and Barbara hold the view that nudity and sex are too often confused, especially by twenty-first century media. Rather, we should be comfortable in our own nakedness for what it really is. Without clothes we are each ourselves, it is not nudity *per se* but what we wear or how we decorate ourselves that turns us into an object of our own or someone else's sexual fantasy.

When John Rogers arrived to photograph the couple for the *Radio Times* a family conference had taken place to ensure that the Pollard children were comfortable with their parents appearing naked in print. Their daughter explained that she was already hardened to peer group comments by virtue of what her parents did wear, never mind what they did not, so it was unlikely that anything new could hurt her.

The press quickly connected the former Abbey site with activities in the nude. 'Would you Adam and Eve it?', ran the headline in the *Daily Mail*, beside one of John Rogers's photographs. When the *News of the World* published more of them, visitors proffered clippings for Ian and Barbara to sign. This was followed by a television stint as 'The Naked Gardeners,' live on ITV's 'This Morning'. Studio sessions were shot with Ian and Barbara behind carefully placed pots of plants whilst the crew went through acrobatics to keep the camera angles within the limits of permitted daytime broadcasting. Eventually, stick-on leaves made the crews' lives less stressful. Television had come rather late in the season, so there were only three appearances before gardening was taken off the morning agenda, but not before the couple had filmed a session, set to music, on location at Westonbirt Arboretum's plant centre; and another session at Abbey House Gardens. This meant putting large notices at the entrance advising visitors to return on another occasion if they felt uncomfortable with nudity. No one turned away. In the gardens of Abbey House, it seemed the most natural thing in the world.

And there was more to come.

Late in 2004 a television production company researcher came to visit. He was looking for participants for a programme to be called, 'Going to work naked'. Several useful facts about Ian and Barbara and their operation resulted in their selection for this programme. First and foremost there was still much heated debate about nudity in public continuing under their roof. Barbara's mother was not sure she approved and their three children had to be considered. Thus the views of three generations could be revealed in a photogenic setting with a public as well as a private life.

The resulting programme was aired for the first time in February 2005. The Pollards' story was juxtaposed with that of three others whose daily lives also incorporated being nude. It was clear that their fifteen minutes' air time could not possibly broach all the

The Naked Gardeners

left: The Waterfall, viewed across the Monastic Fishponds

below: The Wooded Walk to the River Gardens

issues the couple had debated on the subject so Barbara suggested they revisit their 'Naked Gardener' website, registered to avoid potential abuse of the name, and use it as a forum for further discussion. This done, the most common question was from wellwishers asking to visit the gardens in the nude.

This was unexpected but Barbara was prepared to look into it. She approached the Central Council for British Naturism. A former chairman, a retired police officer, would visit and advise on procedure. A date was set, the local police informed, the immediate neighbours contacted for any suggestions as to how to improve the day from their point of view. Season ticket holders were advised by letter, but this proved counterproductive to efforts to keep the press at bay, which was Barbara's preference. A local resident and journalist for a regional paper learnt of the proposal and wrote a story that was picked up by the wider press. Barbara was taken aback; she had wanted a low-key occasion with low-key ramifications.

Cameras had been banned from the gardens on the day but then Barbara received a phone call from the agency of David Modell, a well-known photographer who was also a BAFTA award-winning filmmaker. A look at his website confirmed the excellent quality of his work and its socio-political content. The ban was lifted for him but visitors were made aware of his intention to publish photographs in a book on Middle England. Anyone wishing to avoid the camera had only to make their wish known.

What the Pollards had not realised was that their Clothes Optional Day (or COD as it would become known) was a first for people without clothes to be in the company of people with clothes on a 'public' occasion. Naturist events around the country protected members by making their events entirely without clothes, with the result that a couple could not attend together if he liked to be without clothes but she did not, or vice versa. Abbey House Gardens did not make this distinction and so the non-participating member of a couple had the opportunity

to reconsider his or her view, having now experienced a naturist occasion firsthand and met some of the other attendees.

The press was not to be kept at bay. They were admitted for the first hour only. A press release was given to them, willing subjects for a photo shoot were found, the PR officer for the Central Council of British Naturism made a statement; with their needs met the press left, with the exception of a local television broadcasting unit allowed to stay longer for exclusive interviews with Ian and Barbara. There were still a couple of radio interviews to do live over the telephone but eventually the day would unwind and owners and visitors alike were allowed to relax and enjoy the late summer sun.

News reports were widespread reaching Mexico and Australia, and even a cruise ship in the Mediterranean. All were favourable and a subsequent live broadcast on Australian radio resulted in a coach party booking a visit to the gardens all the way from Sydney.

And so it was that on August 19, a Friday in 2005, the COD went ahead in beautiful sunshine, despite a forecast of rain. Almost eighty per cent of the 275 visitors who made their way to the gardens that day removed their clothes at some point, some for the first time in public. Many who were unable to make the trip because of other commitments, or who were put off by the forecast of rain have asked to be informed of future dates. The Pollards have gladly agreed to arrange more and details will be posted on their website.

The overwhelming memory for Ian and Barbara is of smiling faces, making new friends, and a happy buzz in the atmosphere. Malmesbury shops entered into the spirit of the day with suitably undressed mannequins in their windows. One of the florists offered Swiss Cheese Plant leaves in three sizes, 'modest,' 'average,' or 'blessed,' as an alternative fig leaf. Indeed the local community of Malmesbury took the whole matter in its stride and with great good humour.

They are well used to the Pollards by now.

Ian and Barbara behind the
Viper's Bugloss in the Herb Garden

A Tribute

When asked why we do the garden as we do there probably isn't a simple answer. Many people seem to think that if they had the land they would probably build a wall and keep people out! This book tells you the facts, briefly, of how Abbey House Gardens came into being, but the processes in Ian's brain that gave him the dream and the drive are difficult to put into words. Certainly it harnesses many of his interests and his lifelong answer to many questions is 'Why Not?' If he can't find a reasonable answer to that he will go ahead. But essentially in order to succeed you need to know what needs to be done and looking at the success of others can influence the way. We would like to pay tribute to those who have influenced Ian.

PEOPLE

Adam & Eve — Whether mythical or mystical still a source of inspiration.

David Attenborough — One of the most inspiring of people for all things natural.

Francis Bacon (1561-1626) — Philosopher and Gardener. His most quoted phrase 'God Almighty first planted a garden. It is indeed the purest of humane pleasures and the greatest refreshment to the spirits of man; without gardens, buildings and palaces are but gross handiworks.'

W.J. Bean (1863-1947) — Author of *Trees and Shrubs Hardy in the British Isles* in five volumes, now in its eighth edition.

William Beckford (1760-1844) — For the sheer audacity of Fonthill Abbey in Wiltshire (sadly paid for by slavery) enclosed within a wall 12 miles long by 12ft high, an avenue 100ft (30m) wide by 1 mile long and 22 miles of driveways.

Alan Bloom (1907-2005) — For a new way of thinking about herbaceous planting.

E.A. Bowles (1865-1954) — A truly great gardener who, when completely blind, could still identify a plant merely by tasting a leaf.

Christopher Brickell — For editing the indispensable RHS encyclopaedias.

'Capability' Brown (1716-1783) — Probably the greatest destroyer of England's finest gardens but to be respected for his use of water.

Beth Chatto — A truly inspiring gardener, renowned for her 'Dry Dams' and 'Woodland' gardens.

Nicholas Culpepper (1616-1654) — Herbalist who described the College of Physicians as a 'company of proud, insulting, domineering doctors whose wits were born about 500 years before themselves.' There are over 250 separate editions of his famous *Herbal*.

Charles Darwin (1809-1882) — For revealing the evolutionary links between plants.

M.A. Dirr — American horticulturist whose brilliant encyclopaedias are an inspiration.

John Evelyn (1620-1706) — Gardener and writer. His major work *Sylva or a Discourse on Forest Trees 1664* was written because England was running out of oak trees to build its ships.

John Gerard (1545-1926) — The greatest herbalist of all time. *His Herbal or General History of Plants* published in 1597, describing 2,850 plants is still in use.

Antoni Gaudí (1852-1926) — The unique Spanish architect whose work is so organic he should have been a gardener.

Mrs Grieves — Compiler of the indispensable *A Modern Herbal*, 1931.

Hillier Family (1840-today) — Created the largest (and best) tree and shrub nursery in the world, providing us with many wonderful plants.

Penelope Hobhouse — Has produced more excellent garden books than anyone else.

Henry Hoare (1705-1785) — Creator of Stourhead in Wiltshire. One of the most picturesque scenes in the world.

Thomas Hill (1540-1570) — Author of the first gardening book in England. *The Profitable Art of Gardening* (1563) followed by *The Gardeners Labyrinth* (1577).

Geoff Hamilton (1936-1996) — Everybody's gardening hero. 'The more people I can get to garden, the better the world will be.'

Gertrude Jekyll (1843-1932) — Supposedly inspirational for her collaboration with Edwin Lutyens but does not inspire Ian.

Roy Lancaster — Gardening expert *extraordinaire* who as a curator of the Hillier Arboretum was instrumental in *The Hillier Manual of Trees & Shrubs* surely the most indispensable reference work for gardeners. Ian's original copy from 1974, although very muddy, is still going strong.

George London (pre 1618-1714) — Amazing nurseryman and garden designer who makes Ian feel weak just thinking about him. He rode up to 60 miles a day 'to give directions once or twice a year in most of the noblemen's and gentlemen's gardens in England.' He started Brompton

Park Nursery (now the site of the South Kensington Museums) supplying many thousands of trees to form the great landscaping schemes such as Chatsworth and Blenheim, and also Windsor, Kensington Palace, and more.

John Loudon (1783-1843)	He sought to popularise gardening as an artist to improve the human condition. He started England's first agricultural college, founded *The Gardeners Magazine* (1826) and was the designer of England's first public park. Definitely a hero.
Sir Edwin Lutyens (1869-1944)	Great architect; great garden designer.
Richard Mabey	Described as Britain's greatest living nature writer and broadcaster (after Attenborough of course). The only person who with his *Flora Britannica* can make Ian feel guilty about growing anything other than indigenous plants.
Russell Page (1906-1985)	Landscaper whose book *The Education of a Gardener* (1962) is so good that it has been stolen from Ian's library.
Chris Philip	Devised and compiled *The Plant Finder*, which expanded from 22,000 entries in 1987 to 73,000 in 2005-6. The garden could not be managed without it.
Harold Peto (1854-1933)	Best known for his own garden at Iford Manor in Wiltshire.
R. Philips with M. Rix	Photographer and Plantsman who together have produced 23 of the most stimulating plant books on the planet.
Humphrey Repton (1725-1818)	The most practised, imaginative and pain-staking of all advisers on matters of landscape gardening, as exemplified in his before and after images for his famous *Red Books*.
Walafrid Strabo	9th Century monk, poet and gardener whose writings stated 'to grow your herbs well and good, plant them in raised beds with oaken sides.'
Sir Roy Strong	Lovely man, lovely mind, lovely garden – the Laskett.
Graham Stuart Thomas (1909-2003)	Great Horticulturist, passionate about many things but particularly old roses.
Percy Thrower (1913-1988)	Gardener and broadcaster who inspired so many to garden, including Ian.
Alan Titchmarsh	Probably the best loved (and respected) gardener in the world today – certainly Ian's.

PLACES, too, are inspirational:

Britain
Bodnant; Bowood; Cotehele; Glendurgan; Great Dixter; Hampton Court; Hatfield House; Hidcote; Knightshayes; Levens Hall; Sissinghurst; Stourhead; Tresco

Italy
Boboli Garden, Florence; Isola Bella; Isola Madre; Villa d'Este, Tivoli; Villa Lante; La Mortella

France
Chenonceau; Chaumont; Giverney (Monet); Groussay; Versailles; Villandry

Portugal
Conimbriga; Quita do Alao; Castelo Branco; Bom Jesus do Monte; Palacio de Fronteira

Spain
Alhambra, Generalife; Santa Clotilde

Japan
Katsursa; All Kyoto; Nara

PLANTS reflect our own cellular structure – there is much they can teach us. Some of Ian's favourites are:
Alstroemeria; Ariseama (Cobra Lily); Azaleas
Bamboos; Begonias
Camellias; Cannas; Clematis; Conifers (all of them)
Cornus (dogwoods)
Ferns (especially Tree Ferns); Fritillaries; Fruit Trees (general)
Hellebores; Hostas; Hydrangeas
Irises
Lilies
Magnolias; Maples (especially Japanese)
Narcissi
Peonies (especially Tree Peonies); Palms; Phormiums; Penstemons
Rhododendrons
Roses
Trilliums; Tulips

All that accentuates the amazing way that plants have evolved and adapted to their world, not overlooking all the beneficial microscopic life that makes our soil what it is – the bacteria, fungus, springtails, nematodes.

To be continued …

Two free spirits with a passion for plants are creating a magical garden inspired by the past and doing it as nature intended

BBC RADIO TIMES

Abbey House and its gardens is so filled with atmosphere you can hear the babble of history

COUNTRY HOMES & INTERIORS

What started out as a somewhat improbable idea in North West Wiltshire has assumed world status

WILTSHIRE LIFE

This garden is a very special place

WESTERN DAILY PRESS

Ian Pollard has created a magnificent garden on a site rich in history, with traditional roses, mediaeval herbs and monastic fish ponds

COUNTRY HOUSE & HOME

A wonderful garden with a surprise around every corner

Annette & Dave ,Swindon

A truly superb garden. Vision, courage, hard work all paid off

Alan & Jane, Cambridge

Loved the Gardener's World Special but was even more impressed seeing the garden for real

Helen, New Zealand

We visit many gardens in both Britain and Europe and this is the best we've seen

Dr A.S.,Vermont

The prettiest place in England

Mark & Sarah, London

The Naked Gardeners

Acknowledgments

above: **Kian, Rufus, Arushka**

left: **Dora**

far left **Stewards: Liz, Joan, Bob, Joan, Geraldine, Audrey, June, Robert, Cynthia, Avril, Jane and Margaret (not in photograph)**

This book celebrates the ten years since we made the decision to create a garden we hoped would be worthy of public gaze and just as the garden itself has needed other hands than our own to make it a reality, so has this book.

Our thanks primarily must be to our publisher, Andreas Papadakis for his enthusiasm and willingness to produce the book, to Alexandra Papadakis for her excellent, critical eye in page layout and warm support, to Sheila de Vallée for proof reading, text editing and constructive comment.

We are grateful to Bec Wingrave for permission to use the photograph on page 82, to Mark Bolton for the images on pages 20 and 37, and to Rob Peel for his photographs on pages 8 and 94. We would also like to thank Mark Child for his contributions to the text.

The creation of the garden has taken time, money, commitment, determination, sweat and tenacity some of us did not know we had. Our gardener for five years, Martin Roberts, deserves our heartfelt gratitude for his strength, enthusiasm, dedication and humour, all of which were much appreciated.

The public face of our operation could not function without our stewards, whose consistent support over the past six years has kept us going, or Geraldine, without whom we simply would not manage at all.

From the outset Dora, Barbara's mother, has been relied upon in innumerable ways – our thanks to her for always being there.

Last but not least our appreciation goes to our children, Arushka, Rufus and Kian who have no choice but to put up with our obsessive approach to the garden and a distinct lack of holidays!

left: **Abbey House viewed across the River Valley**

Ian & Barbara Pollard

This view of April's tulip display includes
Passionale, Sorbet, Hamilton, Red Shine, Bonanzo